724. 7

724. 7

Building the
New Millennium

Architecture at the start of the 21st Century

Building the New Millennium

Building the New Millennium: Architecture at the start of 21st-Century brings together a selection of the world's most interesting buildings completed since the year 2000. This diverse collection includes stadia, museums, religious buildings, office blocks, a bridge, a parliament building and a Holocaust memorial. Their geographical spread demonstrates the high quality of new architecture worldwide that has been fuelled by a decade of economic prosperity and a renewed appreciation of contemporary architecture. Increasingly, architects are taking more and more international commissions. Governments, companies and institutions from around the globe are all keen to commission 'signature buildings' from internationally renowned architects.

The buildings range from the tiny and simple Brother Claus Chapel, which has room for only a handful of people at a time, to the vast and complex Yokohama International Port Terminal. Some, despite their innovative appearances, have traditional building structures, such as the Scottish Parliament or Japan's Chichu Art Museum. Others, such as the Selfridges Birmingham Department Store have ingenious new structures developed with the help of computers to meet the challenges of their specific designs. Computer-aided design has made it considerably easier for architects to experiment with new shapes and for engineers to find structural solutions for them. Many of the buildings in this book owe much to this novel technology, including OMA's CCTV television centre, a twisted steel skyscraper with a hole in the middle.

The architects featured include both well-established practitioners and relative newcomers. Álvaro Siza's earliest buildings date from the 1960s, whereas Tezuka Architects were founded in 1994. Architects like Foster + Partners are extremely prolific. Others have built comparatively little: most notably, Zaha Hadid, who had years of waiting before seeing a major project built, and Peter Eisenman, who has spent most of his career as an academic.

Architecture is not immune to concerns of the twenty-first century. Ecological factors play an increasingly significant role in building design, demonstrated here in Foster + Partners' 'environmental skyscraper' at 30 St Mary Axe and Grimshaw's Eden Project. Another recurring theme is the 'structural skin', where the primary structure is the building's exterior, rather than a combination of interior and exterior walls and columns. The Beijing National Stadium, whose woven structure inspired its 'Bird's Nest' moniker, elegantly exemplifies this idea. Finally, a fantastic array of materials is used, from the revolutionary new ETFE plastic — which clads the Allianz Arena — to the simple, and more traditional, local stone of the Scottish Parliament. Glass, concrete, stone, wood and metal are all used in ever more startling ways. It is an exciting start to a new architectural millennium.

Cultural and Congress Centre
Ateliers Jean Nouvel

1

2

Luzern, Switzerland
2000

The Cultural Centre occupies a large site on the edge of the lake in Luzern. Planners declined initial designs that involved projecting the building over the water so the building instead uses the lake as its primary feature, drawing it in as part of the design. The multi-functional facilities consist of three main components. A symphony hall is on the east side with a bar and restaurant overlooking the lake. On the west are galleries, restaurants and an auditorium and between them is an adaptable conference hall.

The spine of the building is set back from the shore and the cubic mass is a horizontal profile beneath the mountains beyond. The three principal elements reach out towards the water, divided by channels of lake water set into the polished stone floor and traversed by pedestrian bridges. Concrete doors, dressed with plaster, are controlled with motorized hinges that allow each door to be positioned according to the required acoustics in the echo chamber. The interior decoration is starkly monochrome with stripes of colour provided by the red doors and dark blue seating.

The various components are unified under a cantilevered copper roof that envelops the centre and overhangs the piazza by 20 metres. The reflective underside of the roof is raised clear of the building on three sides, emphasizing the cantilever dramatically and creating a visual feature visible from across the lake. Metal grilles of varying transparency are positioned on the exterior, allowing visitors brief glimpses of the vista and filtering the light that enters the interior. The layering and juxtaposing of vast planes of glass lends the building a further transparency.

1 Centre seen from the lake
2 Exterior in detail
3 Symphony hall
4 Building in context
5 Covered public piazza
6 View to lake from interior
7 Entrance lobby
8 Circulation space
9 Seating in auditorium

3

4

5

6

7

8

Section through building

Site plan

9

Concert Hall
Mansilla + Tuñón Arquitectos

León, Spain
2004

This playful concert hall occupies the south side of a large plaza in León's historic centre. Although conspicuously modern in contrast to the sixteenth-century Monastery of San Marcos nearby, the building responds to the traditions of its environment with sensitivity. Boasting a museum and music venue its purpose is to revitalize the cultural life of this Spanish regional capital.

The white, latticed facade is composed of five horizontal levels that reference a musical score, the vertical rectangular apertures resembling the notes. The apertures are a series of deeply recessed windows of various sizes that capture the daylight and filter it into the internal spaces. The pockets of illumination created by these openings cast changing shadows that animate the entrance foyer behind the facade and echo the way light pervades the nearby Gothic cathedral. The building is composed of two separate wings: the square-facing volume housing three floors of exhibition halls and an angled wing at the east end housing the auditorium.

The public entrance marks the divide between the blocks and a long ramp leads to the exhibition areas. These gallery spaces give the building a purpose beyond musical performances. The auditorium can be adapted for different events with moveable seats and acoustic panels. Lines of cylindrical lights are suspended from the ceiling shells, illuminating the luxurious interior, lined with ribs of dark wenge wood. The darker tones of the auditorium contrast starkly with the luminosity of the entrance and exterior where the light external walls give on to pale wood floors and panelling. Administrative spaces run along the southern edge of the auditorium whilst technical facilities and rehearsal rooms are accommodated underground.

1   Building in context
2   Main facade
3   Timber-clad auditorium
4,5 Details of facade
6   Courtyard area
7   Detail of interior
8   Entrance foyer
9   Detail of auditorium

3

5

4

6

León, Spain
2000

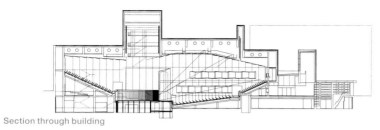

Section through building

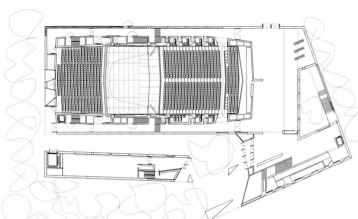

Site plan

7

8

9

13

Parco della Musica
Renzo Piano
Building Workshop

Rome has a new concert hall to rival that of any capital. It takes full advantage of its large site — 55,000 m² (592,015 sq ft) — in the north of Rome, adjacent to a former Olympic village, with three generously proportioned concert halls. The connected buildings form a dramatic ensemble, clustered around a sunken open-air amphitheatre. The design combines the contemporary with the ancient: curved lead-clad roofs over the halls, reminiscent of the bodies of curled-up armadillos, hover over Roman-style red brick bases capped with strips of marble.

There are three halls with varying capacities and a red-brick amphitheatre that seats 3,000. Each hall is designed for a different type of music, so the separation of the volumes makes it easier to isolate the different kinds of sound. The largest auditorium is for large orchestras and choirs; the middle-sized for smaller orchestral concerts, choirs and ballets; and the smallest for more intimate concerts and for contemporary music in particular. Interiors are clad in cherry wood, chosen for its acoustic properties, and are complemented by red seating.

Work on the building was delayed when the remains of a Roman villa were found on the site. These foundations were subsequently incorporated into the design and can be viewed from one of the connecting arms of the largest hall, where there is also a small museum. Other facilities beneath the halls include two large rehearsal rooms, a museum of musical instruments, offices, a library, conference space, lecture theatres, meeting rooms, study rooms, shops, restaurants and cafés. The commercial spaces are housed in the steel, glass and brick arcades at the entrance to the site and the whole 'city of music', as the architect has described it, is surrounded by greenery.

1   Central courtyard
2   Aerial view of site
3   Main auditorium
4   Central amphitheatre
5   Roman villa within site
6   Detail of exterior
7,8   Auditorium interiors

3

15

4

5

6

7

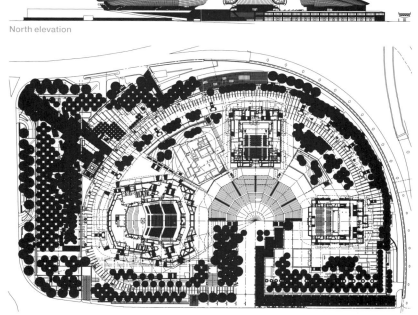

North elevation

Site plan

8

Simmons Hall
Student Residence
Steven Holl Architects

This student residence on the Massachusetts Institute of Technology campus helps to fulfil the college's ambition to pepper their expanding site with unique contemporary architecture. Occupying an unusually long narrow site, the slender footprint leaves room for outdoor public spaces, including a new landscaped pocket park near the entrance, and tree-shaded dining areas in a rear garden and along the southern street edge. Conceived as a continuation of the urban environment, the structure reflects light during the day and glows internally at night, creating a focal point for student activity on what was previously a car park.

The building's concept was to appear porous like a sponge and its form is pitted with over 5,000 small windows. The cast concrete exoskeleton is clad in anodized aluminium and five large apertures are cut out of the perforated facade. These chasms roughly correspond to main entrances and outdoor activity terraces and interrupt the street-like grid of corridors with unexpected openness. Inside are housed communal lounge areas that allow the students to interact, characterized by walls of curving bare cement and amorphous plaster shapes. Externally, these holes break up the monotony of the otherwise uniform block.

The accommodation within includes various amenities for the students such as a 125-seat auditorium and night café as well as 350 bedrooms. These are each equipped with nine operable windows, deeply recessed to provide shade from the summer sun while allowing the lower winter light to warm the rooms. The heads and jambs of these windows are painted in primary house colours, lending an element of brightness to the otherwise monochrome building. Five curving atria cut through several floors like chimneys, allowing air to move about the interior and bringing natural illumination down from roof lights above.

1,2 South facade
3   Communal area
4   View from southwest
5   Detail of facade
6,7 Student living spaces

3

Simmons Hall Student Residence
Steven Holl Architects

4

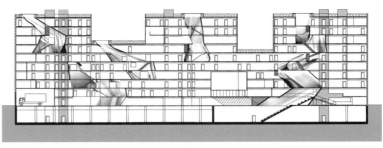

Section through building

Eighth-floor plan

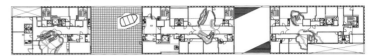

Second-floor plan

5

6

Yokohama International Port Terminal
Foreign Office Architects

This stopping point for cruise ships is a radical addition to Japan's second largest port. From the air it looks more like a park than a building, because of the public promenade on its roof, which is surfaced in timber decking and grass. Foreign Office Architects' starting point was to analyse the circulation of people through the planned building. The result is a design that channels people through an ever-changing sculptural landscape that blurs the distinction between inside and outside.

The visitor access road divides into three, with the central section continuing up a ramp to the drop-off point on the upper level and the main public areas. Two roads on either side form the entrance and exit routes for the car park on the lower level. In addition, pedestrians can walk up ramps onto the roof to enter the arrivals and departures halls or a public hall at the tip of the pier. Long ramps are also used inside the building to connect different levels.

The prefabricated steel structure rests on an existing 400 m (1,312 ft) long concrete pier, acting as both structure and skin, like a ship's hull. Fittingly, it was constructed in shipyards and brought to the site on barges. On either side of the main building there are overhanging sections where up to four ships can dock. The huge column-free halls have metal-mesh corrugated ceilings, which further emphasize their size, with customs areas, check-in, shops and cafés positioned round their sides. The hall at the end of the pier is terminated by a long, glass viewing wall looking out to sea. The rolling roof deck reflects the changing nature of the internal spaces beneath it, while inside and outside are further linked by a continuity in the use of materials: hardwood floors, steps, ramps and sloping walls with steel handrails seem to flow through walls of glass.

1 View from northeast
2 View from south
3 Interior pedestrian ramp
4 Aerial view of terminal
5 Detail of glazing
6 Passenger walkways
7 Covered car park
8 View of interior

3

4

5

6

7

Ground-floor plan

Second-floor plan

21st-Century Museum
of Contemporary Art
SANAA

1

Kanazawa, Ishikawa Prefecture, Japan
2004

This museum sits in the middle of landscaped grounds in the city of Kanazawa. The brief requested a welcoming and inclusive building. The simple and ingenious solution is a circular building with a curved glass perimeter wall that allows people to see what is going on inside; glimpses of internal activity that will encourage visitors to venture in and explore for themselves.

The museum offers a new way of experiencing art: galleries are contained in discrete volumes in the centre of the building, each surrounded by circulation space that extends to the circumference and opens up to incorporate the public gathering places. The building can be entered from a variety of points at ground level, or from the car park on the subterranean level, which also houses storerooms and a small auditorium.

Incorporated into the outer ring are a lecture hall, children's art studio, lounge, art library, shop, café and offices. Where these areas are enclosed, the walls are made from frameless glass. In order to accommodate a wide variety of artwork in all kinds of media, the nineteen exhibition rooms come in different shapes and sizes and have varying ceiling heights, with the taller galleries protruding from the flat roof on the outside. The flexible nature of the layout enables ticketed exhibitions to use as many or as few rooms as they require. Situated between the galleries are four fully glazed courtyards that bring daylight into the centre of the deep plan.

The colour palette is simple, with slender white columns supporting the roof, white walls, and polished and unpolished concrete floors.

1   Aerial view
2   Museum illuminated at night
3   View of entrance
4,5   Details of glazed exterior facade
6   Interior courtyard

21st-Century Museum of Contemporary Art
SANAA

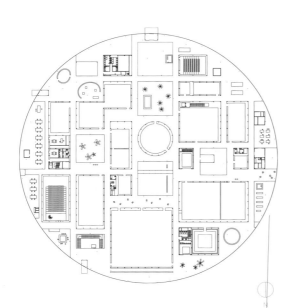

Ground-floor plan

2

3

4

5

6

Braga Stadium
Souto Moura — Arquitectos

1

2

The Braga stadium, inaugurated for the 2004 UEFA Championships, occupies a former quarry beneath the Monte Castro hills near Portugal's ecclesiastical capital. The site is unusual, with a sheer granite cliff on one border and open space on the other, but this high, rocky terrain was necessary to avoid flooding. The structure responds to the landscape with a theatrical form that dominates the environment and is unique among sports venues in offering natural scenery in such close proximity to the playing field.

Unusually, there is no seating at the goal ends of the pitch. Instead, it is consolidated into two cantilevered grandstands with two overlapping tiers. This simplified layout enhances the view from the stands and eliminates the seats where the outlook might normally be limited. The northeast stand is dug directly into the hillside, the rock excavated from its foundations reused in the concrete superstructure. The opposite stand leans away from the field on struts that resemble the ribs of a ship. Circular apertures perforate the thick concrete to reduce the sense of mass and create the impression of transparency. The exposed structure and stairs have a strong sculptural presence. Freestanding concrete troughs at the roof edges carry rainwater away down hillside channels and add to the sculptural character of the stadium.

Shade is provided by lightweight ribbed metal panels suspended from parallel tensile cables that extend over the space between the stands. These were modelled on the suspension bridges that the Peruvian Incas used to span river gorges and they provide a translucent view of the sky above. Concrete columns support the pitch from below and the void beneath houses the circulation spaces, car park and players' facilities. Daylight filters down through a metal grid bordering the field above.

1   View of pitch
2   Building in context
3,4 Details of concrete structure
5   View from pitch
6   Detail of site
7   Circulation space
8,9 Exposed staircases

3

4

5

6

7

8

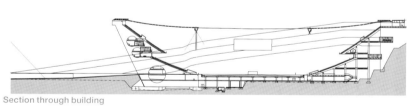

Section through building

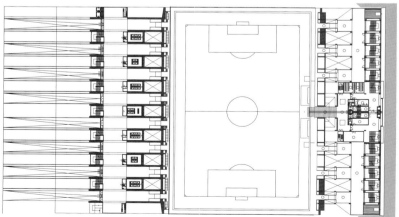

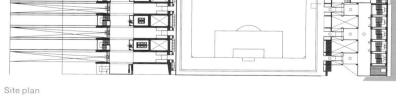

Site plan

9

Matsunoyama Natural Science Museum
Tezuka Architects

1

2

Situated in a remote mountainous region north of Tokyo this natural science museum provides exhibition spaces and research facilities dedicated to the examination of the rich local ecology. The region can be subjected to snowdrifts as deep as 7 m (22.9 ft) and the extreme weather conditions are a primary factor influencing the form of the building. The heavily armoured structure, built to resemble a ruin, must withstand snow loads of up to 2,000 tons (4,400,000 lbs). Its industrial appearance is in stark contrast to the minimal glass and steel constructions typically associated with contemporary Japanese architecture.

Externally, the building is reminiscent of an industrial building, with a low-lying body and snaking footprint that follows the topography of the surrounding hills. An observatory tower at one end rises above even the deepest banks of snow. The museum's irregular bulk is clad with steel plates that can expand and contract in response to the intense changes in temperature. This material was also chosen for the alterations in its colour that would take place over time and the rusted patina that it would acquire.

Encased inside the textured armature, the entrance leads past meeting rooms and laboratories to the exhibition hall and café that inhabit a meandering white tube running through the centre of the building. Huge picture windows, made of thick acrylic, are placed in the bends of the passage, offering views into a cross-section of the snow in winter. The changing light and colours that filter in through different depths create an unusual atmosphere. The tower provides a further sensory experience as visitors climb the steps in a semi-darkness punctuated by a light and sound installation powered by solar panels on the roof.

1   View from south
2   East facade
3   Main entrance
4   View from southeast
5   View towards observation tower
6   Detail of exterior
7,8 Lecture and exhibition spaces

3

Matsunoyama Natural Science Museum
Tezuka Architects

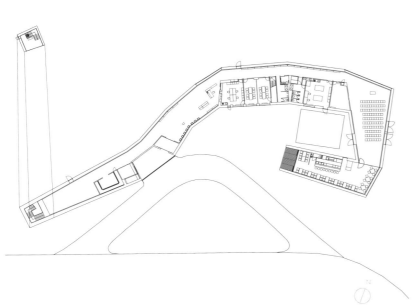

Ground-floor plan with axonometric of tower

4

5

Tokamachi, Niigata Prefecture, Japan
2003

6

7

8

Lois & Richard Rosenthal
Center for Contemporary Art
Zaha Hadid Architects

1

2

3

4

Cincinnati, Ohio, USA
2003

This arts centre in the middle of Cincinnati is Zaha Hadid's first completed commission in the USA. The building, with its facade of protruding and receding box-shaped volumes and its sloping ground plane, which extends out into the street, is typical of Hadid's work. It's a novel addition to a conventional street of traditional shops and office buildings, designed to draw in a diverse range of visitors, some of whom might not ordinarily visit galleries.

The facade at ground level is fully glazed and the pavement outside gradually rises up to a centrally placed entrance, beneath the overhanging galleries. Inside, the floor of the high-ceilinged foyer continues to rise until it reaches the rear of the building, where it curves up sharply to form the back wall. A glazed

shaft in front of this wall contains staircases that zigzag up to the top floor. From this transparent stairwell visitors can see into the galleries and out to the city. An underground performance space can also be seen through slits cut in the foyer floor.

Galleries, stores, exhibition preparation areas, offices, an education centre and a café are housed over the six floors stacked on this narrow site. Rather than employing a repetitive floor plan, the interior spaces are composed from interlocking volumes that play with levels and sightlines. Galleries come in different shapes and sizes for different scales of work and exhibitions. Externally, galleries are expressed as concrete and matt black aluminium-clad solids, in contrast to the offices and public

areas, which are glazed. This enables the offices to be lit naturally and the light in the exhibition spaces to be controlled.

1   View from across street
2   Building in context
3   Detail of exterior
4   Atrium interior
5   Detail of exterior
6   Gallery at ground level
7,8 Interior circulation spaces
9   Detail of stair ramp
10 View of stairs from above
11 Atrium interior

39

5

6

7

8

9

10

11

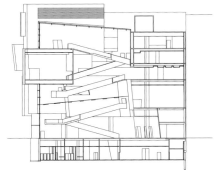

Section through building

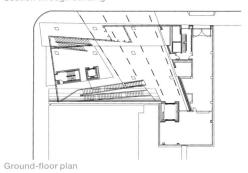

Ground-floor plan

Selfridges Birmingham
Department Store
Future Systems

1

2

This startling, curvy, dark blue building covered in shiny metal discs is a state-of-the-art Selfridges department store in the heart of Birmingham. It follows in the footsteps of the first Selfridges, on London's Oxford Street, which was a ground-breaking building in its day. It is part of a larger complex that replaces the 1960s Bull Ring shopping centre in an attempt to stimulate urban regeneration. Future Systems are famous for their organic shapes, which they model in Plasticine during the early stages of design.

The shop forms the end of one arm of the new shopping centre and is bounded by a railway station, a nineteenth-century church, a new plaza and a multi-storey car park. The aluminium-studded exterior is punctured by bands of glazing on the ground floor and the occasional yellow-framed curved window higher up. An enclosed glass bridge stretches out from one of these windows and over to the car park. On the roof a restaurant opens out onto a central kidney-shaped roof terrace, which has at its centre the glazed ceiling of the atrium that rises up through all four shop floors, with shiny white escalators soaring up through the space.

The building's structure met the challenge of creating a curved shell without incurring high building costs. A conventional steel structure supports the floors, and these in turn support a facade of concrete sprayed onto metal mesh. This concrete shell is thick enough to hold its own shape without the need for a supporting structural frame. The 15,000 metal discs fixed to the concrete surface disguise what is essentially a very innovative building made of concrete.

1,2   Views of exterior showing raised entrances
3   Escalators in atrium interior
4   View of exterior at night
5   Detail of outer surface
6   Detail of entrance bridge

3

4

Birmingham, UK
2003

Section through building

Site plan

5

6

Walt Disney Concert Hall
Gehry Partners

1

2

Frank Gehry employs his repertoire of swooping wave-like forms to full effect in the Walt Disney Concert Hall, the new home of the Los Angeles Philharmonic Orchestra. It is a mass of curving steel sitting askew in the centre of its site, in marked contrast to its neighbouring office blocks, which follow the city grid.

The hall and surrounding gardens are built on a raised platform on a sloping site. A flight of steps leads up to the main corner entrance but most people enter the main lobby via the red escalator that emerges from the car park beneath. A central rectangular box — the auditorium — is screened on the outside by waves of steel that appear to peel away from glazed walls. A number of smaller sculpted volumes express different functional spaces, such as rehearsal rooms, a restaurant, a flexible area for pre-performance entertainment, lavatories and circulation spaces. The founders' room, next to the main entrance, stands out by virtue of its shinier steel cladding and its many petals reaching upwards. Behind the auditorium, a smaller 250-seat theatre with an undulating steel entrance canopy is sunk into the six-level parking structure. Above it, on the raised garden level, sits an open-air amphitheatre.

The main auditorium has a capacity of 2,265. Concave and convex balconies and stalls, clad in Douglas fir, contain brightly coloured seats. Behind the stage, under the billowing timber roof, sits a dramatic set of enormous organ pipes. Windows and skylights let in natural light where the roof canopy recedes at the two end walls. Spaces between the auditorium and outer shell provide spill-over areas for the audience during intervals. These foyers and the orbiting rooms have curved white plastered walls and bursts of sculptural timber columns.

1,2   Views from the street
3   Interior of main auditorium
4   View of exterior at night
5   Detail of exterior
6   Outdoor amphitheatre
7   Concert hall lobby

3

4

5

6

7

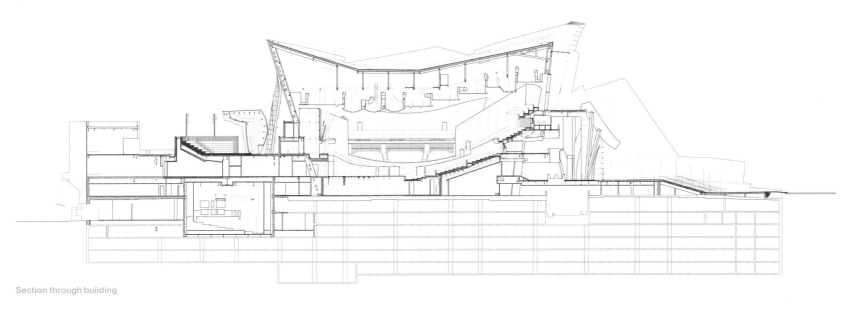

Section through building

30 St Mary Axe
Foster + Partners

1

2

3

4

London, UK
2004

30 St Mary Axe is one of a new breed of tall buildings in the financial district of the City of London. Nicknamed the 'Gherkin' because of its distinctive bulging conical shape, it has already attained iconic status in the capital. As a highly engineered and environmentally advanced building, it follows in the footsteps of other Foster buildings such as the Commerzbank (1997) in Frankfurt, Germany.

An innovative diagonally braced structural steel skin is clad with approximately 5,500 diamond-shaped glass panels set into aluminium frames. The load-bearing outer shell frees up the floor plan from structural columns, allowing it to be used more flexibly. Triangular glazed atria twist as they rise through the building, maximizing natural light in the interior. They are terminated by an unbroken floor plate every six floors and the bases of each atrium can be used as an informal meeting space. The 41 storeys provide 76,400 m² (822,362 sq ft) of commercial office space, a shopping arcade on the ground floor, and a private bar and restaurant in the roof. This room, which occupies the whole of the top floor, has the only curved piece of glass in the building — the lens at the summit of the tower — and an uninterrupted 360-degree view of London.

Environmental awareness was the determining factor in the design. The ergonomic shape reduces wind around the base of the tower and enables the windows onto the atria to be opened. The form also creates external pressure differentials, which means that air is forced in a particular direction in order to drive a unique system that ventilates 40 per cent of the building naturally. The tapering base has a further advantage: at ground level the building appears smaller than it is and space is made available for a street-level public plaza.

1   Exterior view at night
2   Detail of facade
3   Building in context
4   Private dining room on 40th floor
5,6 Details of diamond shaped glazing
7   Main entrance
8   Interior circulation space

51

30 St Mary Axe
Foster + Partners

5

6

7

Elevation

Sixth-floor plan

Ground-floor plan

Casa das Mudas Art Centre
Paulo David

A man-made plateau crowning a volcanic basalt promontory towering 180 m (600 ft) above the Atlantic, the Casa das Mudas Art Centre is a multi-purpose cultural venue on Madeira's west coast. Appearing initially to be an inaccessible mass, the centre unravels on approach to reveal a labyrinthine series of internal and external spaces. The building is formed of two intersecting blocks of the local black basalt that echo the stepped agricultural terraces typical to the rural area in which the adjacent sixteenth-century Casa das Mudas is placed.

The external stone surface is scored with rows of planters and deeper incisions formed by walkways, light wells and sunken patios. The visitor is initially ushered down a ramp to a central patio, open to the sky, with access to a restaurant, museum, library, bookshop and auditorium. A structure of concrete mixed with steel beams to span larger voids, enables the construction of a descending sequence of four double-height galleries. Narrow stairwells inhabit the thick walls between the exhibition spaces and connect the galleries. These open onto expansive halls with sudden glimpses of the distant ocean vista, oscillating between senses of claustrophobia and freedom.

Daylight is introduced to two of the galleries through high-level windows that filter illumination into the lower levels. White walls and floors of Brazilian garapa wood are complemented with horizontal strips of warm fluorescent lighting.

The bright artificial glow provided by carved tube-lit handrails set into the sturdy walls accentuates the sense of compression in the stairways. At night, low-level lighting embedded in the basalt lights up the ramps and stairs, and the central patio glows through its semi-opaque glazed panels.

1   Building in context
2   Terraced roofs
3   Main courtyard at night
4   Cliff-top observation point
5,6   External walkway
7,8   Gallery interior
9,10 Double-height interior spaces

3

Casa das Mudas Art Centre
Paulo David

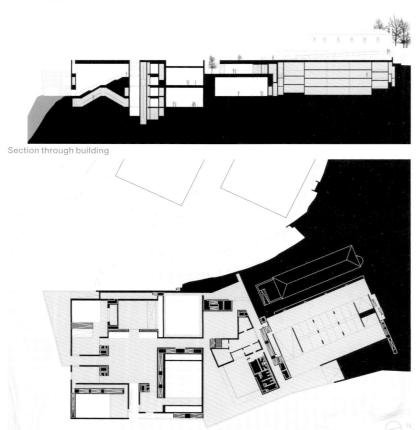

Section through building

Site plan

4

5

6

7

8

9

10

Chichu Art Museum
Tadao Ando Architects & Associates

The Chichu Art Museum houses a permanent collection of works by three artists: the Impressionist painter Claude Monet and contemporary artists Walter De Maria and James Turrell. It is built into a hill surrounded by salt-pans on the island of Naoshima.

The design expands on a subterranean theme that Tadao Ando explored in an earlier gallery built on the island. In this building the whole of the reinforced concrete structure is buried in the grassy hill, which is pierced with exposed courtyards, passageways and chambers covered by skylights. These are all simple geometric shapes. The lack of external superstructure is deliberately disorientating, thereby encouraging the visitor to focus on the artwork. These plays on views, the exposed rough concrete and the careful use of light and shadow are typical of Ando's work.

The approach to the building is along a ramp leading to an entrance wall in the hillside. A tunnel leads through the hill and into a square, submerged, concrete-lined grassy courtyard. From here, a staircase winds up around the perimeter to an entrance lobby. A long, concrete-lined outdoor corridor connects this entrance and administration wing to the upper level of a three-level gallery wing. At the end of the corridor there is a triangular courtyard covered in rough stones, beyond which is a series of gallery spaces. The three works by Turrell are located in interconnecting rooms on the middle level of one side of the triangular courtyard. On the lower level, on an adjacent side of the courtyard, De Maria's sculptures are arranged on a broad, bare concrete staircase beneath a gently curved concave ceiling. The paintings by Monet are hung in a white-walled and white-mosaic-floored room beyond, on the middle level. Further on, a café and the director's office are stacked on top of each other, with views out of the hillside.

1   View from building
2   Building in context
3   Triangular courtyard
4   Detail of concrete-lined corridor
5   Recessed courtyard
6,7 Interior gallery space

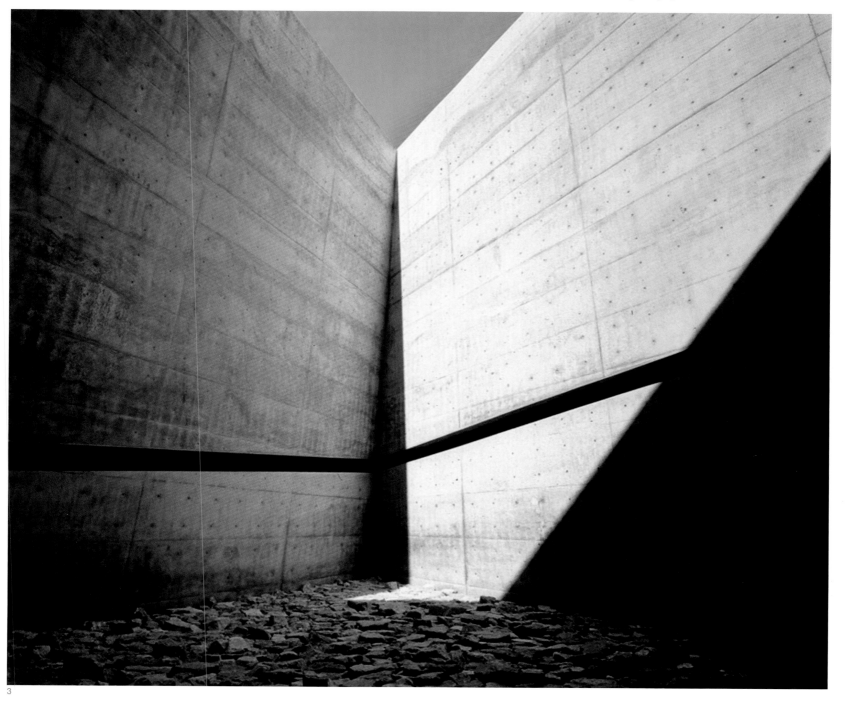

3

4

5

6

Section through building

Floor plan

7

Henze and Ketterer Gallery
Gigon/Guyer Architekten

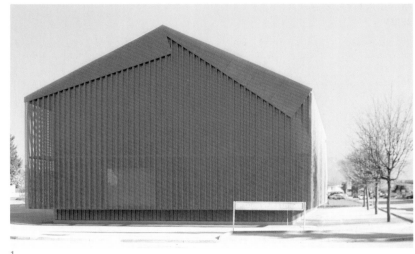

1

2

This multi-purpose art store and gallery is located on a curious bell-shaped site to the southeast of Bern. Providing a secure and stable repository for contemporary works of art, the building also enables visitors to view objects not currently on public display in the owner's main gallery, and offers a space for small temporary exhibitions. Perhaps inspired by the drama of the surrounding Swiss landscape, the design employs a juxtaposition of translucency and opacity to give the barn-like structure texture.

The building is divided into three distinct environments: a basement store, a ground level gallery with loading bay and a loft with an open floorspace for displays. The accommodation is connected by a lobbied service core near the entrance that contains a lift, stairs, lavatories and a kitchen, providing a space-efficient solution to circulation around the building.

Local planning regulations dictated that the depot echo the form of the local farmhouses neighbouring the site with a pitched roof. The plot boundary determines its twisted footprint, maximizing the amount of floor space offered by the awkward site whilst leaving room for car parking. Constructed entirely of concrete, the building is heavily insulated throughout in order to maintain the optimum storage temperature for the art works. The facade is clad in metal sheeting with an outer layer of ribbed and perforated panels in greyish blue.

These provide necessary shading to the windows but also add movement to the exterior. At the peak of the roof, solid metal sheets fold over the trapezoidal ridge to create a smooth triangular apex. Embracing the hillside ordinances, building codes, coastal laws and design review boards, the building strategically transforms these stringent criteria into a sculptural and efficient architectural solution.

1   Building in context
2   View from southeast
3   Gallery interior
4   Main entrance
5   North facade
6,7 Details of exterior

3

4

5

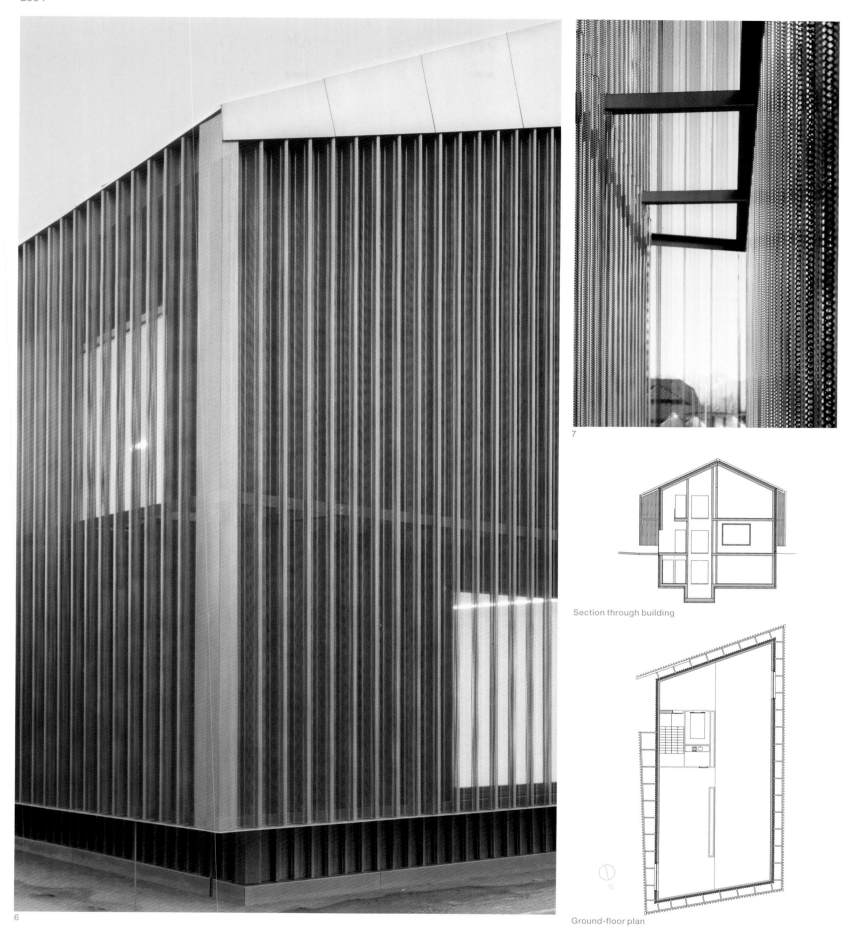

7

Section through building

Ground-floor plan

6

Millau Viaduct
Foster + Partners

1

2

The Millau Viaduct, currently the tallest bridge in the world, crosses the Tarn river in southern France and completes the motorway linking Paris to Barcelona. The old road wound laboriously down the side of a wide gorge between two plateaux and through the town of Millau, resulting in gridlock in the summer months. After exploring different options, architect Norman Foster and bridge engineer Michel Virlogeux hit on the dramatic solution of spanning the whole 2.5 km (1.5 mile) width of the gorge. Their design is a pared-down structure that curves and slopes as it crosses the gorge.

Seven bare concrete columns spaced 342 m (1122 ft) apart range in height from 75 to 253 m (246 to 830 ft) and support a dual carriageway with safety reservations on each side. Above the road level the concrete columns become white steel columns and rise a further 90 m (295 ft). To accommodate the expansion and contraction of the road caused by changes in temperature, each column is formed as an A-frame above the road level and splits into two thinner columns below the road. These then merge into one column again before sinking into the ground. Eleven tension cables on either side of each column fan down to the centre of the road to help hold it up. On either side of the road transparent aerodynamic side screens shelter vehicles from high winds.

The bridge was constructed using tall temporary steel towers between the columns to take the weight of the cantilevered road sections before they were connected. Work could be carried out on all seven columns simultaneously by hydraulic rams, using GPS to ensure they were correctly aligned. Once the road sections were connected, the masts and cables were installed and the temporary supports removed.

1   Bridge in context
2   Aerial view
3   Detail of aerodynamic side screens
4   Bridge surrounded by clouds
5   View from bottom of gorge

3

67

4

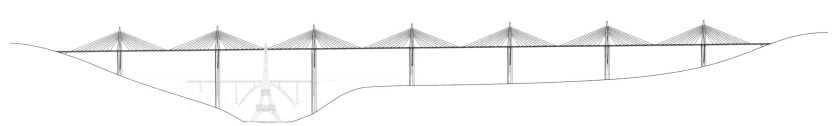

Elevation

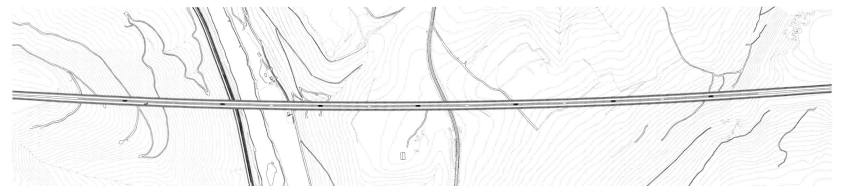

Site plan

5

Scottish Parliament
Miralles Tagliabue—EMBT

1

2

Scotland's new parliament building is situated on a 9.9 hectare (4 acre) site at the foot of the Royal Mile, the historic street that stretches downhill from Edinburgh Castle. The Catalan architect Enric Miralles won the commission with a design that focused on the relationship between the building, its site, the country and its people. Democracy is a central theme and there is a deliberate lack of hierarchy and ceremonial grandeur. This is most apparent in the flowing shapes of the volumes and the consistent use of locally sourced high-quality materials in both public and private areas.

A collection of buildings with concrete, steel and laminated-wood structures form a loose U-shaped plan. On the west edge of the site is a long office block for the Members of the Scottish Parliament (MSPs). Inside, each cell-like office has a 'thinking' window seat, which overhangs the facade. On the outside, strips of oak and granite screen the windows, resulting in a textured and colourful repetitive motif. To the north, along the Royal Mile, the seventeenth-century Queensbury House sits beside a new block with an impenetrable blastproof wall inlaid with chunks of Scottish stone on which quotations from Scottish literature are engraved. At the east end of this wall is the MSPs' entrance with a protruding triangular concrete volume above.

A long canopy marks the public entrance to a foyer with a sculptural concrete ceiling. Above, an elliptically shaped, wood-lined debating chamber has a roof supported by an elaborate network of oak beams and stainless-steel wires. In the centre of the complex, four leaf-shaped towers house offices and vaulted committee rooms. Tying all the disparate elements together, and acting as a meeting place for MSPs, is an airy court with rooflights wrapped in stainless-steel panels.

1   View from landscaped garden
2   Glazed roof over main concourse
3   Debating chamber
4,5   Details of exterior
6,7   Exterior facades
8,9   Views of interior
10   'Thinking' window seat

3

4

5

6

7

8

9

10

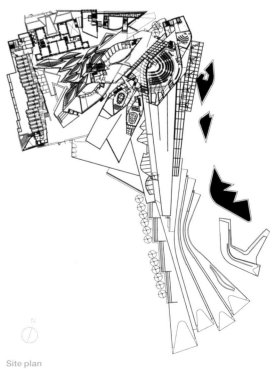

Site plan

2

3

Utrecht, Netherlands
2004

A new addition to Utrecht University's 1960s campus, Wiel Arets' library aims to draw a more diverse audience to the site. A masterplan was devised in the 1980s to renew and add to the university's existing buildings, and this library is one of a succession of completed buildings in the scheme. Providing space for the storage of over four million books, five reading rooms, an auditorium, exhibition area, café and offices, the building attempts to provide a secure and comfortable resource for students and the public.

The building has the outward appearance of an inviolable monolithic block of black texturized concrete. The facade is punctuated by grey glass panels decorated with a silk-screen design based on a photograph of willow trees by the Dutch photographer Kim Zwarts. This transparent skin filters the light admitted to the interior and offers views of the building's internal volumes. A meandering set of steps leads visitors into the library where the interior functions of the building now reveal themselves.

A cavernous void rises through the six-storey space, which is filled with floating concrete cubes for book storage. Suspended from these are platforms that accommodate the various reading areas. These structures divide the interior into various zones connected by stairs and slopes creating a combination of narrow lanes and open spaces. The monochrome colour scheme of the exterior continues inside with polished black ceilings and a glossy grey floor. The black is intended to promote concentrated study in the vast chamber while the floor is reflective enough to illuminate the white tables sufficiently for reading. The red reception counters, the lounge seating and the books themselves impart the only elements of colour.

1   South facade
2   Southwest corner
3   Book shelving space
4   Northwest corner
5   Reading room
6   View across central void

4

Sections through building

Site plan

5

6

Allianz Arena
Herzog & de Meuron

1

2

This 66,000-seat football stadium on the northern edge of Munich provides a new home for two teams — Bayern Munich and TSV 1860 — who previously shared the 1972 Olympic stadium. Its bubble-like form rises out of an open, grassy landscape. The wraparound plastic shell of the building is used to ensure that the stadium feels like home to whichever team is playing: it can be illuminated in the colours of each respective home team — red or blue — or remain a neutral, incandescent white.

A processional route to the stadium begins with winding asphalt paths on the landscaping above subterranean stacked parking. The glow of the lit-up exterior filters through to the stands, which provide an unobtrusive grey canvas that is animated by the coloured strips of the fans. Unlike the old stadium, there is no athletic track separating the three ranges of seating from the pitch. Each tier is steeper than the one below, which creates excellent sightlines and a lack of hierarchy. The hole in the roof is sized to ensure that the optimum amount of daylight reaches the pitch.

The exterior of the stadium is made from diamond-shaped ETFE (ethylene tetrafluoroethylene) pillows. ETFE is a plastic that weighs less than 1% of the equivalent quantity of glass. The air-filled cushions, which vary in size from 4 to 8 m (13 to 26 ft) long and 2 to 4.25 m (6.5 to 14 ft) wide, are held on a steel frame of cantilevered trusses. This external cladding and the seating are supported in turn by the concrete structure, which contains the circulation spaces and function rooms.

1   Aerial view
2   View of illuminated shell
3   Stadium interior
4   Stadium at night
5   Parking spaces underneath entrance walkway
6   Concrete staircases to stands
7   Detail of external shell

3

4

5

6

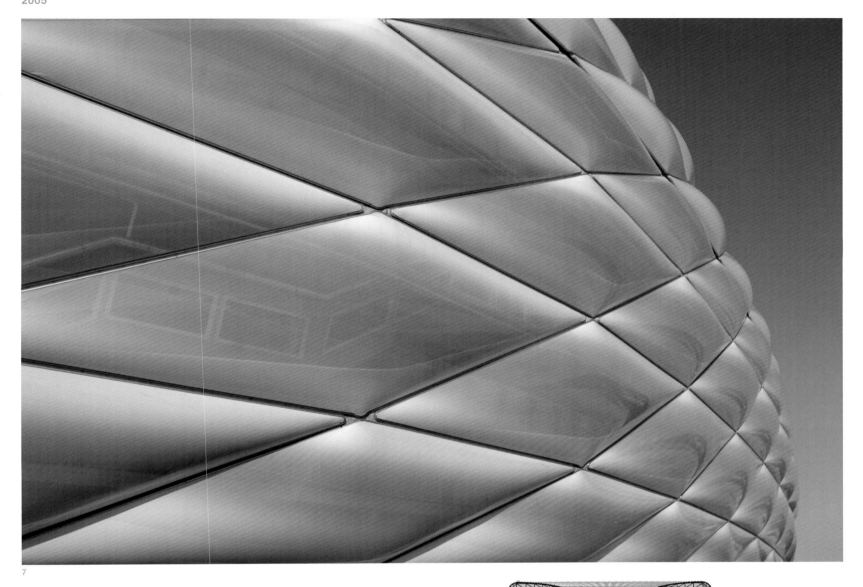

7

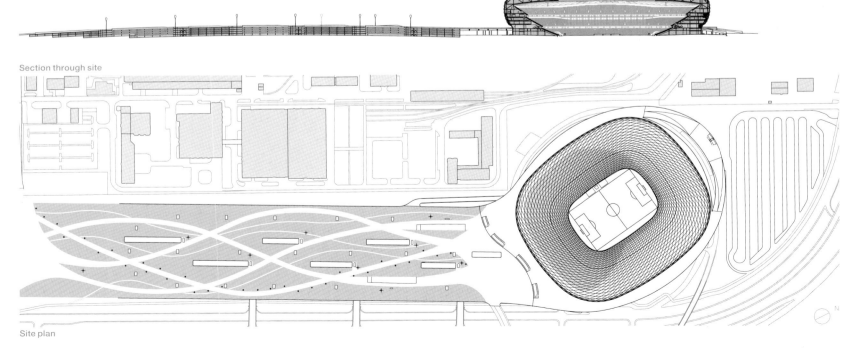

Section through site

Site plan

Casa da Música
Office for Metropolitan Architecture (OMA)

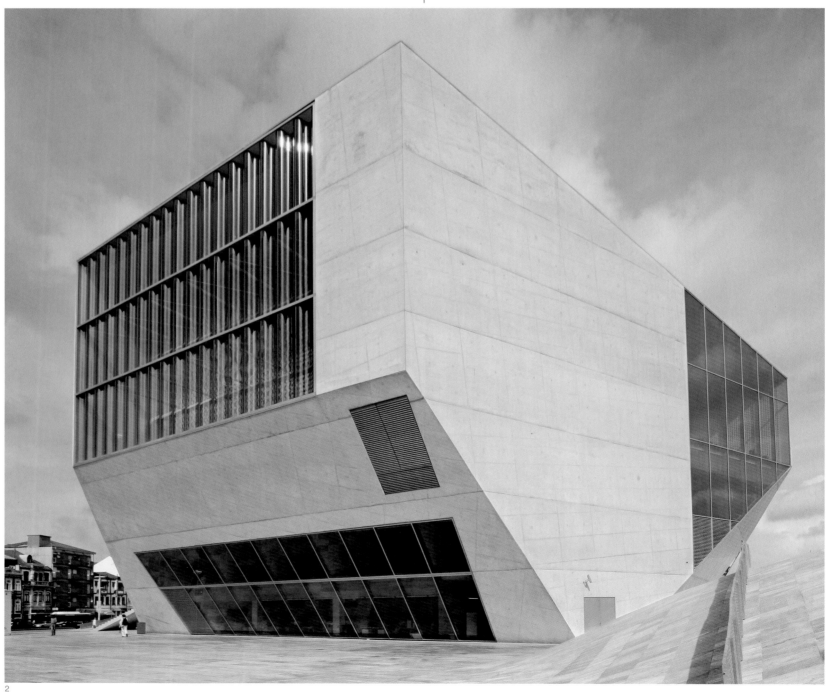

This concert hall is a multifaceted mass of diagonally scored white concrete and glass positioned at the centre of its own pink travertine-paved, undulating landscape. It sits in contrast with the surrounding cityscape of the old town of Porto, where building-lined streets radiate from the Rotunda da Boavista — a large roundabout containing a park. The venue caters for fans of classical, rock and pop music, and provides a home for Portugal's national orchestra.

A broad flight of stairs leads to a raised public entrance. Inside, a twisting aluminium-lined staircase rises through the angular space that hugs the central hall. The hall itself is illuminated by shafts of light that are filtered through diagonal concrete beams. A continuous public route formed of stairs, platforms and escalators takes the visitor up and around the building. This connects auditoriums, public rooms, rehearsal rooms, dressing rooms, recording studios and educational facilities, and culminates in a restaurant, where a chequer-tiled terrace is recessed into the roof.

Good acoustics dictated rectangular shapes for the two auditoriums. Both concert halls have glazed walls constructed from a double layer of acoustically engineered rippled glass where they meet the outer skin or where they collide with other performance rooms. The idea of the auditorium as an enclosed box is turned on its head with the creation of this visual link between the audience and the city outside, and between the different performance and social spaces inside. The building's 40 cm (15.5 in) thick outer shell and the two 1 m (3.5 ft) thick internal walls of the main auditorium combine to form the main load-bearing structure, which is braced by floor plates. In contrast with the severity of the exterior, the interiors are highly coloured, with an enlarged gold-leaf wood-grain pattern in the main hall.

1,2 Building in context
3 Grand auditorium
4 Public entrance to building
5,6 Staircases forming route through building
7 View from VIP room
8 Small auditorium
9 Roof terrace

3

Casa da Música
Office for Metropolitan Architecture (OMA)

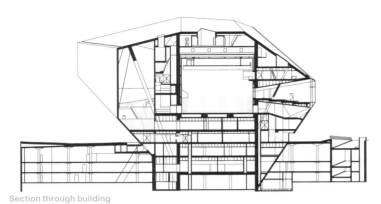

Section through building

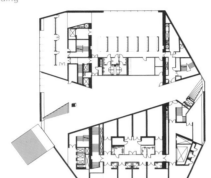

Ground-floor plan

4

5

6

7

8

9

Eden Project
Grimshaw

Bodelva, Cornwall, UK
2005

The Eden Project houses plants from around the world in climate-controlled greenhouses. Situated in the southwest of England, its vast domes are sheltered in a disused china-clay pit. The original design for the domes was based on Nicholas Grimshaw's building for Eurostar at Waterloo Station, which was a wide-span glazed structure. However, this was soon rejected because of the uneven terrain of the site, and geodesic domes were employed to solve the problem of the varying ground levels. The result is an unforgettable, futuristic building.

Two connected greenhouses or biomes, one for humid tropical plants and one for warm temperate plants, are composed of eight overlapping bubble-like structures on either side of a green-roofed entrance building. The structures are between 18 and 65 m (59 and 213 ft) wide to accommodate the varying heights of the plants. The domes are made from a double layer of hexagons composed of straight, galvanized steel tubes, bolted to each other by cast steel nodes. The shell action of the intersecting domes provides structural stability. The cladding comprises triple-layered inflated ETFE (ethylene tetrafluoroethylene — a high-tech plastic) pillows, which are transparent and lightweight, and can cover wide spans with minimum support. Coloured lights illuminate the domes at night.

A number of smaller buildings surround the biomes. There are two aluminium-roofed volumes perched on the edge of the crater: a visitor centre with a rammed earth wall, and an administrative building. Down below, alongside the biomes, there is a shell-shaped education centre with a spiky copper roof. Every building on the site is designed to be energy-efficient and incorporates local building materials and techniques where possible.

1,2   Aerial views of site
3   Detail of biome structure
4   Biome from above
5   Biome roof from interior
6   Visitor centre roof

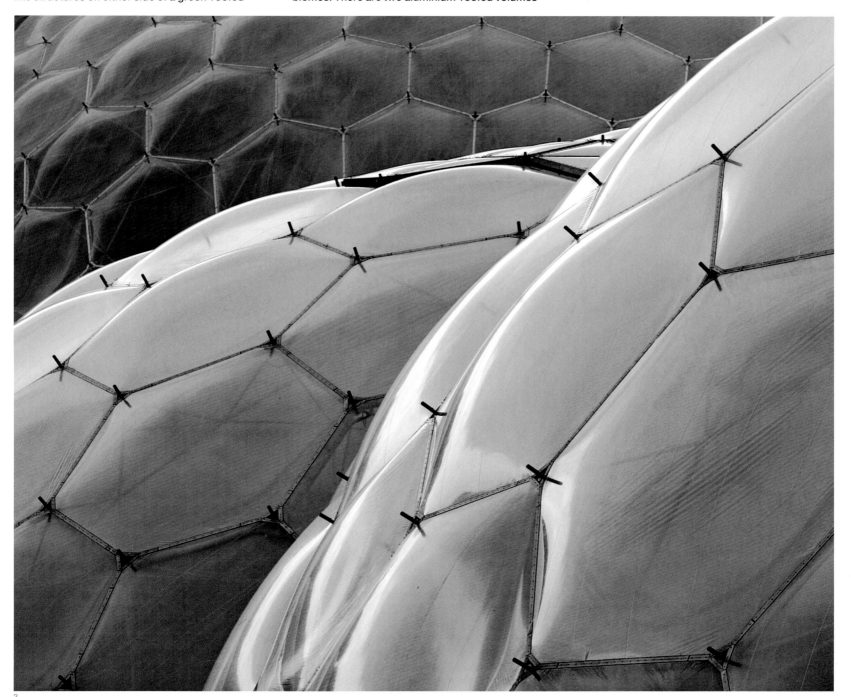

3

4

Site plan

5

Memorial to the Murdered Jews of Europe
Eisenman Architects

1

2

This long-awaited memorial attempts to represent the magnitude and horror of the Holocaust. It is in the middle of the north–south strip running through the centre of the city where the Berlin Wall used to be, and is surrounded by office buildings, apartments and a park. A vast sea of grey stones rises up out of the land to stop passers-by in their tracks. The orderly layout of concrete pillars marching into the distance is an expression of the dullness of the bureaucratic system that underpinned the Holocaust and represents the thousands of individuals who suffered its brutality.

A rigid north–south grid structure is composed of 2,700 concrete pillars, or stelae, each 95 cm (3.1 ft) wide and 2.5 m (8 ft) long, with varying heights up to 4 m (13 ft) and spaced 95 cm (3.1 ft) apart. They are not all quite straight, giving the impression that they are tilting in the wind. The narrow gap between them forces people to walk in single file, which gives a feeling of solitariness and encourages silent contemplation. The rise and fall of their heights is echoed in the artificially created undulating ground plane. At the edge of the site the stelae are only very slightly raised above ground level, but towards the centre they rise up; the ground falls away and they become dark and imposing. The straight lines of the grid allow views to the city beyond but sounds are muffled, allowing space for reflection.

A small subterranean visitor centre lies at the southeastern corner. Coffered ceilings in the four main galleries reflect the pattern of stelae above ground. Illuminated displays tell the story of Jewish persecution by the Nazis and a database contains further information about individuals affected by the Holocaust. No lists of names appear on the stelae above ground: they are left to speak for themselves.

1   Detail of stelae
2   Aerial view of site
3   Visitor centre interior
4   Detail of stelae at ground level
5   Visitor centre exhibition space
6,7 Illuminated exhibition displays

3

4

Section through site

5

6

7

National Assembly for Wales
Richard Rogers Partnership

1

2

The National Assembly for Wales is prominently located overlooking the Bristol Channel in the former dockland area of Cardiff Bay roughly a mile from the centre of the Welsh capital. The building is a striking addition to the locality, an area that embodies the city's quest for regeneration and national identity. Although relatively modest in scale — the Assembly comprises only sixty members — the building has a temple-like presence. This is partly due to its elevation atop a plinth clad with local slate, which lifts the building above pedestrian level and allows light to penetrate the low level administrative offices.

Externally, the main body is made up of a dynamic transparent glazed latticework of steel meant to symbolize democratic values of openness and participation. The building is dominated by its huge undulating red cedar roof, which shelters both interior and exterior spaces. A 'wind funnel' pierces the roof, descending through the upper public gallery and emerging above the debating chamber, serving the dual purpose of conveying daylight into the room and providing natural ventilation. An environmental agenda is present throughout the design; the thermal bulk of the slate pedestal regulates internal temperature and deep bore holes in the ground act as a cooling mechanism.

Approaching the building, the spectacle of the billowing roof and the multitude of steps ascending the platform create a noteworthy entrance. A large public foyer encompasses the upper level and includes an elevated viewing area from which visitors can peer down on the political proceedings below. The subterranean assembly chamber is a large circular space at the heart of the building, defined by its dramatic cyclonic roof formation.

1,2   Main facade
3   Assembly chamber
4   Public plaza
5   Cantilevered roof
6   Main entrance
7   Foyer
8   Detail of roof
9   View of roof from chamber

3

4

5

6

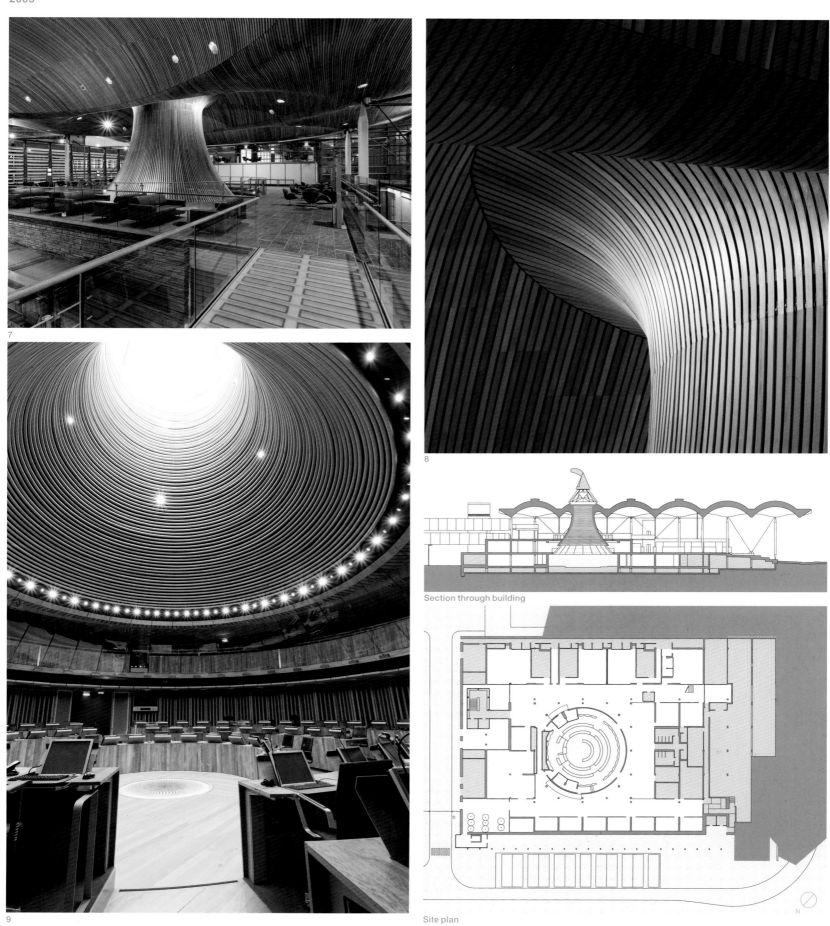

7

8

9

Section through building

Site plan

Novartis Campus — Forum 3
Diener & Diener Architekten

1

2

This arresting office block signals the entrance to a new campus for a pharmaceutical company's headquarters on a site next to the Rhine. Diener & Diener collaborated with artist Helmut Federle and architect Gerold Wiederin to design the jewel-like exterior of the building, and this is combined with a thoughtfully planned interior to make a truly exceptional workspace.

Coloured-glass panels cover the whole of the exterior, with the exception of the entrance wall on the ground floor, which is recessed by 8 m (26 ft). Metal clamps extend from polished, chrome-plated steel rods that hang from the roof to support the frameless glass panes, which are formed from sheets of glass sandwiched together for added strength. Three layers of rectangular glass of varying sizes are arranged in no particular pattern. In places the panes overlap, creating different colour effects, and occasional gaps between panes are spread across the facade. Balconies stretch around the block on the four upper floors, separating the glass from the inner, enclosing, clear glazed wall.

The ground floor has a central foyer and lounge with meeting rooms on either side. The lounge, with its wall of glazing that can slide open in the summer, reflects the ethos of the company and provides an informal meeting space and relaxation area for staff. Three concrete stairwells support the concrete floors and steel framework of the upper levels. The floors above contain a mixture of small offices and larger open-plan spaces, incorporating meeting rooms and refreshment areas. Deep balconies on the north and south facades and a conservatory at the west end of the building provide further spill-over office spaces. The muted tones of the interior materials, such as the polished brown limestone floors, cream leather upholstery and American walnut veneer, contrast with the exuberant exterior.

1,2	Exterior views of building
3	View of interior work space
4	East facade
5	Detail of staircase
6	Glass meeting space
7	Internal garden

3

5

6

7

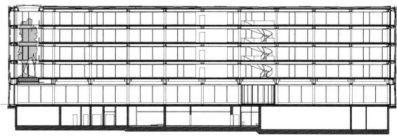

Section through building

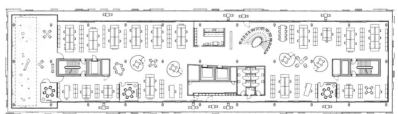

Third-floor plan

Ground-floor plan

Schaulager Laurenz Foundation
Herzog & de Meuron

1

2

The Schaulager, or Viewing Warehouse, is a repository dedicated to the conservation, research and dissemination of contemporary art. This unconventional project provides spacious storage for the Emanuel Hoffmann Foundation's collection of artworks by over 150 artists, including pieces by Klee, Dali and Delaunay, and is primarily intended for specialist use by curators, students and academics. Built in a suburb of Basel, the facility is expanding the city's cultural and public dimension southwards towards a new district. Durable and solid, the design is a combination of innovative technology and Swiss geometric practicality.

Externally, the building resembles a vast bunker with concrete facades clad with gravel excavated for the foundations. The material of these walls is a visual expression of weight and storage, and this sturdiness assists with internal climate control, helping to maintain an optimum temperature for the works. Daylight is admitted through carved fissures in the heavy walls, designed to imitate the shape of the unearthed pebbles on a large scale. One side of the box-like form is indented to create a forecourt leading to the entrance. This is guarded by a small gatehouse with a gabled roof, reflecting the local architecture in which domestic buildings are juxtaposed with massive industrial sheds.

Inside, the atrium ascends the full height of the building and presents a cross-section of the various spatial levels. This vestibule leads into temporary exhibition spaces on the ground and lower-ground floors accompanied by a café, bookshop, auditorium and two permanent art installations. The alabaster plaster ceiling of the cafeteria undulates like the roof of a cave and enhances the artificially natural appearance emulated throughout. The three upper levels comprise flexible storage space in which the artworks are kept in densely arranged display cells.

1   Visitor entrance
2   View from northeast
3   Entrance lobby
4   View from southwest
5,6 Details of facade
7,8 Auditorium and gallery spaces

3

4

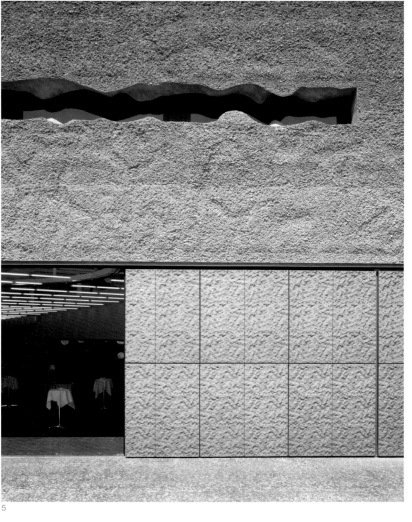

5

6

7

8

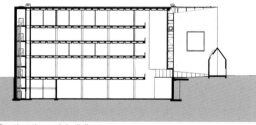

Section through building

Ground-floor plan

Shipping and Transport College
Neutelings Riedijk
Architecten

This new Shipping and Transport College is aptly sited on the edge of Rotterdam's harbour. It is a groundbreaking design for an education facility and looks more like a contemporary office block, albeit an unconventional one. This is no coincidence as the college has close ties with the administrative side of the shipping industry and the building houses a number of maritime consultancy firms.

A central tower has two large protruding horizontal volumes attached to it, one at the top and one at the bottom. The volume at the bottom contains most of the larger communal spaces such as the dining halls, sports hall, lounge and media centre. The tapering vertical part of the building is 70 m (229.5 ft) high and contains the classrooms. These

are linked by escalators in bright red shafts that allow the students to move quickly between floors during class changes. Open areas interspersed between the classrooms provide recreation space for the pupils. Staff rooms and offices fill the top floors and the upper protruding volume, which leans out 20 m (65.5 ft) over the ground floor restaurant, contains a 300-seat auditorium.

The architects took their inspiration for the contorted shape of the building, and for the pattern of the facade, from the cranes and silos of the surrounding port. The grey and blue checks of the cladding are made from corrugated metal sheets and cover every surface, breaking only to give way for bands of glazing, and give the impression of

stacked containers. Walls of windows in the leaning section at the top and in the restaurant at the bottom provide panoramic views out over the river and to the sea in the distance. These viewing walls feature in a number of Neutelings Riedijk Architecten's buildings, including the fire station in Breda and office building in Amsterdam.

1   View across harbour
2   Cantilevered top level
3   Lecture hall
4   Building in context
5,6 Details of interior
7   Internal escalator
8   Lower-level restaurant

3

4

5

6

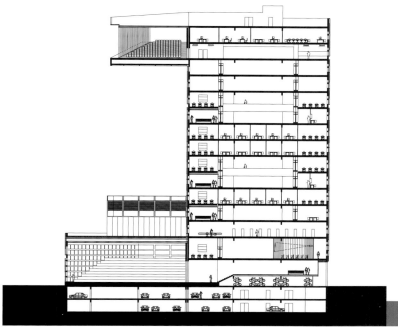

Section through building

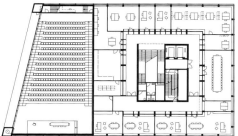

Fourteenth-floor plan

7

8

Terminal 4, Barajas Airport
Richard Rogers Partnership

1

2

This new terminal doubles the capacity of Barajas Airport's capacity and establishes Madrid as a major transport hub. More than a million square metres (over 10 million sq ft) of buildings, including parking structures and a new metro, are designed to handle 35 million passengers a year. 'Our aim has been to create an airport that is fun, with lots of light, great views and a high degree of clarity,' says Richard Rogers. He has achieved this by keeping the planning simple and covering the whole terminal and a satellite building with an undulating lightweight bamboo roof, supported by a colourful steel structure.

The modular structure of the two main buildings is formed from regularly spaced, M-shaped steel roof beams that curl up at the ends, which are supported by central, Y-shaped steel beams on concrete columns and two peripheral, diagonal steel rods that are anchored to the ground. The aluminium-covered roof has broad overhangs at the facade, with diagonal shades to protect the glazed perimeter wall from the sun. The exposed steelwork is painted in a range of hues that change from red at one end, to yellow in the middle and blue at the other end.

Inside, the overall impression is of a light-filled building dominated by the rising and falling of the pale bamboo ceiling with its circular rooflights. The painted steel structure adds to the feeling of warmth and the changes in colour throughout the approximately 1 km (0.6 miles) long buildings help orientate passengers. Airport facilities are distributed over six floors: three above ground for passengers and three underground for services and a connecting shuttle train. The stages of passenger processing — arrival, check-in, passport control, security checks and departure — are contained in parallel sections separated by cavernous light wells that maintain a sense of light and space.

1   West facade of terminal
2   Detail of exterior
3   Check-in areas
4,5 Terminal gates
6   Passenger thoroughfare
7   Baggage hall

3

4

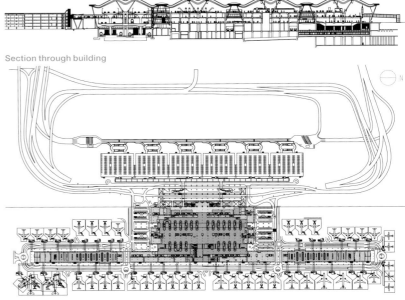

Section through building

Site plan

5

6

2005

113

Torre Agbar
Ateliers Jean Nouvel

Barcelona, Spain
2005

This contemporary interpretation of a skyscraper in multi-coloured glass and concrete soars above the rooftops of Barcelona's city centre. The Torre Agbar's shimmering solidity is a startling contrast to the filigree spires of the city's other vertiginous landmark, Gaudi's Sagrada Familia. An office building that is reminiscent of Foster + Partners' 30 St Mary Axe in London, its striking appearance and innovative structure set it apart from its environment.

Inside, the building is designed as a free-flowing space although the low ceilings and small windows create a confined atmosphere at odds with the exuberance of the exterior. An innovative structure of reinforced concrete walls that taper towards the pinnacle supports 35 floors that encircle an asymmetrically positioned central elevator shaft and creates an open, column-free floor space. The oval floor plan allows the occupants greater proximity to the windows, which are concentrated on the north facing side where the glare of the sunlight is less harsh. The interior is lined with colourful storage cabinets that react to the light filtered through the restricted openings and mirror the patterns created externally.

Rising singularly from a calm streetscape, the tower is based on the idea of a geyser erupting, its fluid shape diffused by a membrane of glass louvres. These slats create shade and air movement within, and the 4,500 window openings cut from the structural shell allow the building to be naturally ventilated. The surface is clad with corrugated opaque aluminium panels in red, blue and white. These create a blurred, mirage-like effect evocative of fire, water and steam that reinforces the volcanic symbolism. At night, the effect becomes more dramatic as a multitude of LED devices create a luminous display on the facade.

1   Building in context
2   View from north
3   Entrance lobby
4   Detail of facade
5   View across city
6,7 Details of interior

3

115

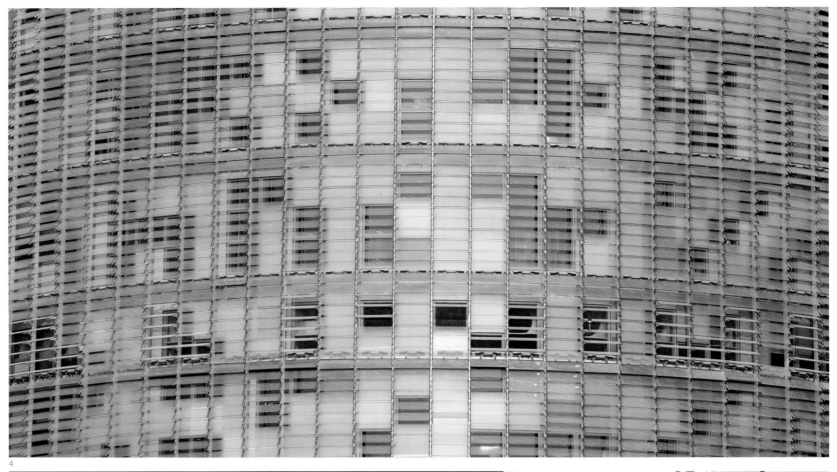

4

5

Section through building

Site plan

6

7

Woerman Tower and Plaza
Ábalos & Herreros

4

Las Palmas de Gran Canaria, Spain
2005

This new residential tower and its companion office block are situated on the narrow spit of land that connects the old and new towns of Las Palmas, with the beach on one side and the harbour on the other. Instead of building on the whole of the large rectangular block, Ábalos and Herreros decided to build upwards to take advantage of the spectacular views afforded by a higher vantage point. This is a building that grows up and out to connect to its locale, which is unusual in a structure of this height.

The accommodation is split into two. The seven-storey office block is on the north side of the site and the 60 m, sixteen-storey tower is on the south. This frees up the central plaza, which is paved in Portuguese stone, for public use. The bulging first

floor of the tower and the recessed ground floor of the office block provide necessary shade, and palm trees form organic walls on the exposed east and west sides. Both buildings have fully glazed facades with dark metal frames and sunshades that wrap around every floor. The colours and shapes employed are derived from nature, such as the randomly placed greenish-yellow glass panes with plant motif patterns and the curved glass in the corners of the buildings. The final touch to the exterior are the leaning top two floors, which are pushed out so that they hang over the plaza.

The architects wanted to design apartments that they themselves would like to live in. This meant high ceilings, views out to the city, sea and mountains,

shadows cast by sunshades and tinted windows. A structural concrete core is aided by slender white painted columns on the perimeter, just inside the glazing. The overall effect is of a sparkling exterior that fits comfortably into its surroundings.

1   Building in context
2   Facade from ground level
3,4 Views of building from street
5   South facade
6   View from beach
7   Base of tower at night
8   Top residential floor
9   Detail of exterior

6

7

8

9

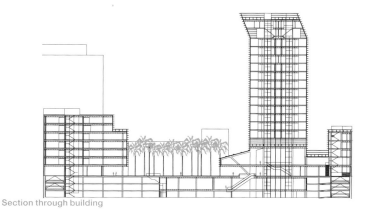

Section through building

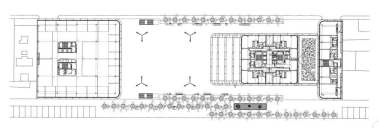

Site plan

Freitag Flagship Store
Spillmann Echsle Architekten

1

2

3

4

Zurich, Switzerland
2006

Freitag's new flagship store is a clever marketing tool, which, in line with the company ethos, reuses existing materials. Situated in Zurich, the hometown of the two brothers who founded the company, the store, constructed entirely from used shipping containers, is aptly surrounded by some of the city's main road and rail routes. Equally fitting is the nature of the company's product — bags made from discarded lorry tarpaulins, bicycle inner tubes and car seatbelts. The inspiration for these came to one of the brothers when he lived in an apartment next to the same lorry route that the shop now overlooks.

The building is formed from seventeen standard, 6 m (20 ft) long containers that were hand-picked in the port of Hamburg and brought to Zurich by rail.

They are stacked in an asymmetrical formation, with a 25 m (82 ft) tower of nine containers rising from a four by two container base. A glazed entrance and four large windows cut into the sides of the vertically stacked display spaces allow views in and out of the building. Steel staircases rise up through the structure to an observation platform at the top of the tower where there are dramatic views of the city, a lake and the mountains beyond.

The containers are stacked and connected with fastener elements used in the shipping industry, although some are slightly modified; 28 mm (1 in) hardwood floors are fixed to the bases of the containers on the lower levels and the combined weight of these helps to lower the centre of gravity

of the building. Recycled glass is used to insulate against the cold of the Swiss winters. The building is expected to have a five-to ten-year life span and will leave only a shallow concrete foundation on the site when it is removed.

1   Building in context
2   View of exterior
3   Detail of container structure
4   Retail space
5   Exterior at night
6,7 Details of retail space
8   Glazed container end
9   Viewpoint on roof

6

7

8

9

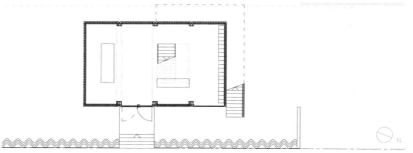

Ground-floor plan

'Meiso no Mori' Crematorium
Toyo Ito & Associates, Architects

This secular funeral hall has a beautiful, serene setting by a lake surrounded by wooded hills. The most striking feature of the building is its gently undulating white roof, which has been likened to snowfall on the hills. The roof is supported by, and blends seamlessly into, downward tapering columns. The building almost seems to be part of the landscape — a theme that Toyo Ito has explored in other buildings, such as the I-Project in Fukuoka.

The 20 cm (7.5 in) thick reinforced concrete roof was designed with the help of the engineer Mutsuro Sasaki, who used computer modelling to establish the most efficient form to cover a set of internal spaces of differing heights with a single canopy. Structural walls at the rear of the building and twelve conical columns with built-in rainwater pipes, some concealed within walls and some exposed, provide seemingly effortless support.

The two storeys at the back of the building, white like the roof, contain the cremation area. There is direct access for staff and vehicles behind, on the south facade. Beside this white box is a marble-clad box containing ceremonial spaces and offices. A slender arm containing a third block is squeezed into the narrow space between the hill and the lake and contains rooms for funeral parties. These internal functions within separate enclosures are surrounded by circulation spaces with seating areas, and everything is contained by the glass perimeter wall overhung by the waving line of the roof. The main public entrance is on the east facade and the roof extends here to provide a canopy for cars. Details such as the curving base of the light-coloured travertine marble wall where it meets the travertine floor, and the curve of the white wall of the cremation hall where it meets the white ceiling, bind the horizontal and vertical elements together.

1 Northwest facade
2 Detail of roof structure
3 Communal seating area
4 Detail of roof
5 Main entrance to building
6,7 Glazed lobby and reception areas

3

'Meiso no Mori' Crematorium
Toyo Ito & Associates, Architects

4

5

6

7

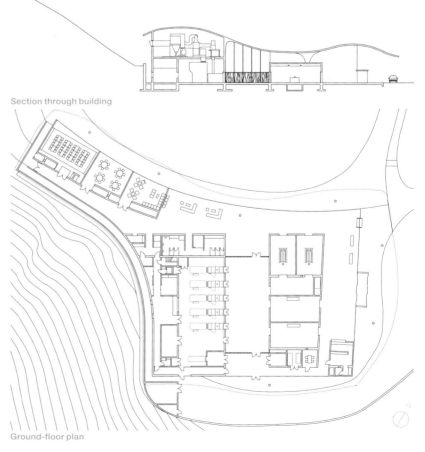

Section through building

Ground-floor plan

Papertainer Museum
Shigeru Ban Architects
+KACI International

The Papertainer Museum is a temporary exhibition pavilion created to commemorate the thirtieth anniversary of the design and cultural media company Designhouse Inc. Located in the Seoul Olympic Park in the suburb of Songpa-Gu, the building's D-shaped footprint is a reaction to the position of existing paths within the surrounding woodland as well as a representation of the name of its patron. Although the building directly responds to its environment in this way, it is nevertheless a recyclable structure that can be dismantled and reconstructed elsewhere. This aspect of mobility adds to the already unique design.

The museum takes its name from its unusual construction materials. The building is formed of 166 steel shipping containers and 353 towering paper columns, supported by a foundation structure of steel beams. The paper used is extremely dense rendering it highly durable and resistant to water and fire. A giant colonnade of paper tubes forms the monumental facade of the pavilion. Behind this, a grid of containers are stacked four high, alternately left open or sealed up to create a chequered pattern of voids and solids. These boxes are used as display booths, offices and storage cupboards. At the rear, more paper tubes shape the curved walls of the semi-circular volume, preventing natural light from entering the space.

The interior is divided into three simple elements. Two exhibition halls provide a vast space for the display of artworks made of recycled materials. The first is the rectangular volume behind the grand facade, accommodating the Container Gallery. This space is flooded with light from large openings at either end. The curvilinear portion of the building is more shadowy and encloses an open-air atrium at the heart of the building, which houses a café and sculpture garden.

1   West facade
2   Aerial view
3   Large exhibition space
4   View from north
5   Exterior facade detail
6   Interior facade detail

3

Papertainer Museum
Shigeru Ban Architects + KACI International

4

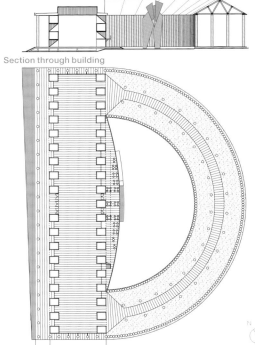

Section through building

Floor plan

5

Ann Demeulemeester Store
Mass Studies

2

Seoul, South Korea
2007

Formerly a residential neighbourhood, Seoul's Gangnam district is rapidly changing into an upmarket commercial district of shops, bars and restaurants. Tucked away behind the primary thoroughfare, this three-storey detached shop houses the collections of the fashion designer Ann Demeulemeester. The building responds to the dense urbanity of its environment with a botanical architecture that brings nature into the city. The impracticality of building a stand-alone structure for just one designer was balanced by the different uses incorporated within the project.

The store is wrapped around a central courtyard and car park that creates an indentation in the centre of the building. The facade of herbaceous

perennials planted into the fabric of the exterior creates a living wall that continues inside. The entire building is clad in this turf and only large panels of glass break the green surface. The transparent main boutique is placed to the west of the courtyard while the stair to the upper floor restaurant and basement multi-store is to the east. The rear and both sides of the building, which border adjoining sites, are surrounded with a thick hedge of bamboo.

The first floor boutique is an organic form apparently carved out of the exposed concrete. The undulating ceiling pours towards the floor in a series of round columns creating arched openings that look out through the tangle of external foliage. Underneath the stairs are housed various services

including fitting rooms, storage spaces and a bathroom. The stairs lead the visitor upwards to the restaurant above. Here, the large main eating space opens onto two outdoor terraces — a hidden rear balcony and a rooftop patio — that provide more intimate spatial characteristics.

1   South facade
2   Retail space
3   Detail of facade
4   Internal living walls
5   Detail of retail space
6,7 Details of staircase
8,9 Staircase at upper-level

135

3

4

5

6

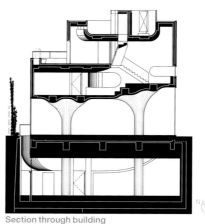

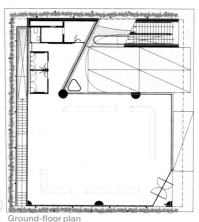

Section through building

Ground-floor plan

7

8

9

Brother Claus Chapel
Peter Zumthor

1

2

Mechernich, Bonn, Germany
2007

Standing alone on the edge of a field, this small chapel is a simple building with a powerful atmosphere. Peter Zumthor is renowned for his spiritual and sensual buildings. He is also very selective about the projects he undertakes and likes to spend time perfecting them. When a farming couple approached him to design a chapel dedicated to Nicholas of Flüe (Brother Claus), a hermit, mystic and political mediator, he agreed to do it for free as a gift for his mother who admires the patron saint of Switzerland.

Zumthor proposed a modest design that could be built by the farmers, their family and friends. The building method is unusual: part construction and part destruction. A wigwam-like structure was made out of 112 tree trunks felled in a local forest. Then every day, over a period of twenty-four days, a 50 cm (19 in) layer of concrete made from locally sourced river gravel, reddish yellow sand and white cement was poured around the trunks. When the concrete was set the trunks were set alight and left to burn slowly for three weeks in a process similar to charcoal burning. Once the fire had subsided, the remaining wood was removed, leaving the walls with charred indentations.

On approach, the sole clue to the chapel's purpose is a tiny bronze cross above the door. The triangular opening is the only way into the irregularly shaped five-sided tower. Inside, a dark narrow passageway with a pointed roof leads to a single room with sloping blackened walls, which culminate in a tear-shaped hole, open to the elements, at the top. The 350 holes left in the concrete from the construction process are filled with sparkling hand-blown glass. A basin in the poured-lead floor collects rainwater, which runs out via a channel.

1 View of exterior from entrance pathway
2 View of interior towards entrance
3 Rear of building
4 Detail of holes in concrete facade
5 Triangular entrance
6 Metal door
7 View of interior upwards to roof opening

Brother Claus Chapel
Peter Zumthor

3

4

5

140

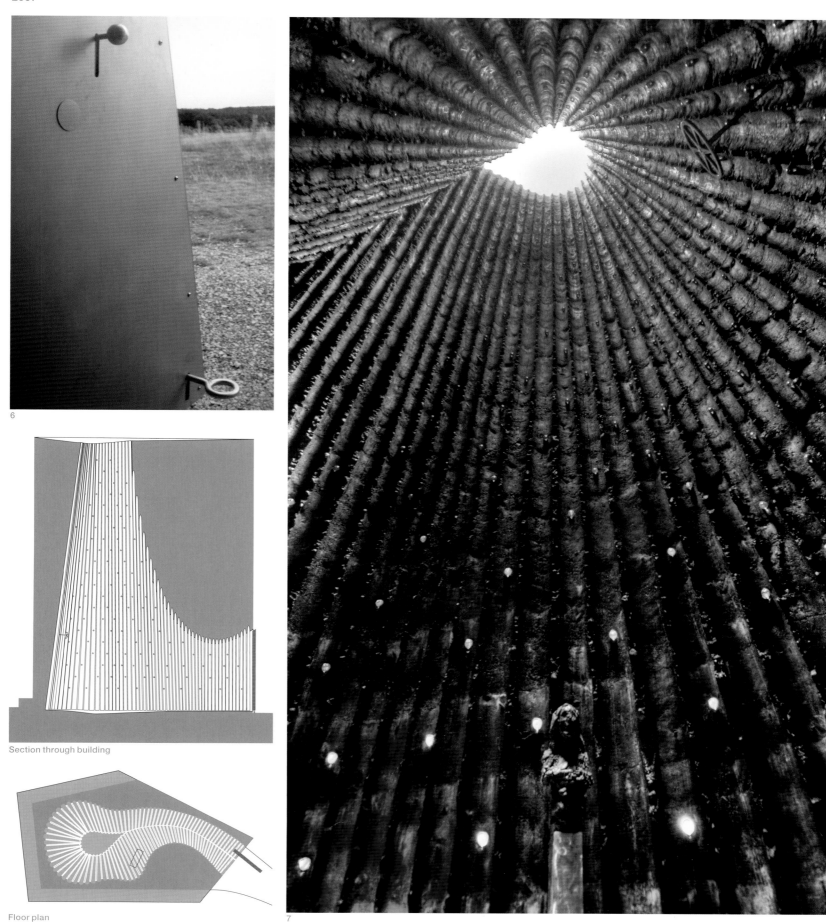

6

Section through building

Floor plan

7

Kolumba Art Museum
Peter Zumthor

1

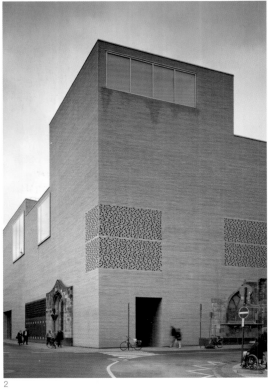

2

3

4

Cologne, Germany
2007

This is an unusual museum on an unusual site. The Kolumba Art Museum of the Archbishopric of Cologne was founded in 1853 by the Society for Christian Art. Its new home is on the site of a Gothic church that was partially destroyed in World War II. In 1949 an octagonal chapel, designed by Gottfried Böhm, was built in the church's ruins to house a statue of the Virgin Mary that had miraculously survived the bombing. Then, in the 1970s, investigations revealed the remains of a Roman building within the church's walls. The new museum incorporates all of these previous structures in addition to providing new galleries for its collections. Swiss architect Peter Zumthor has designed a thoughtful building that combines old and new to provide spaces for

reflection on a collection that spans the same 2,000-year period as the building.

The materials used in the new building are sympathetic to the existing structures. Walls made of thin, light grey bricks, similar to those used by the Romans, are built directly on top of the remaining church walls. They enclose the octagonal chapel and the Roman ruins in a double-height space. A timber walkway winds in and out of concrete-covered slender steel columns that support a bare concrete ceiling. High up in the walls the bricks are spaced apart so that a dappled light enters through the perforated sides.

An entrance foyer leads to the hall of ruins, a courtyard garden and a staircase leading up to

the galleries. The galleries are spread over two floors above the double-height volume, raising the new building above the older ones. Together they comprise the whole of the building's functions, as there are no shops or cafés here to detract from the business of contemplating the art and architecture.

1,2 Street facade
3   Courtyard with church ruins
4   View from gallery space
5   Perforated facade
6,7 Details of interior showing Gothic and
    Roman remains
8   Interior gallery space

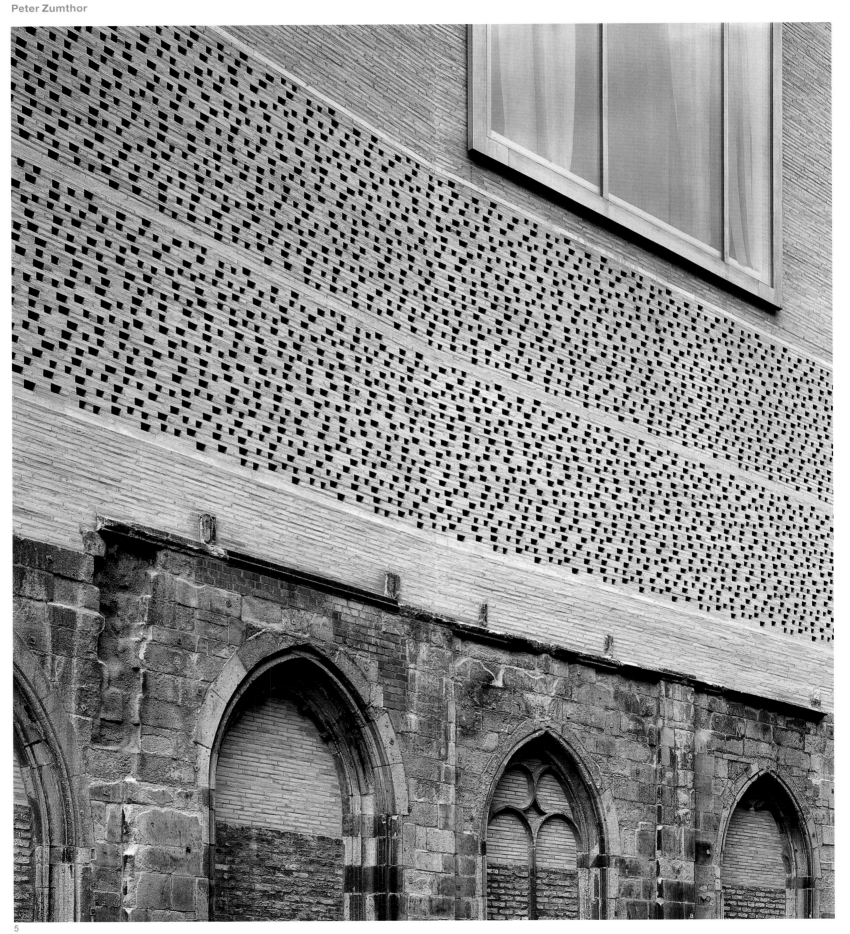

5

6

7

8

CCTV and TVCC
Television Centres
Office for Metropolitan Architecture (OMA)

1

2

China's new television centre is a striking reinter-pretation of the skyscraper. Rather than competing to be the tallest, the architects have experimented with the form. CCTV is a twisting loop with a central hole through which neighbouring towers in the new Central Business District can be viewed. The adjacent TVCC is a more conventional building, which rises from a wide base into a slender tower, and contains public facilities and a hotel. There is also a Media Park on the site, which hosts public events and can be used for outdoor filming.

CCTV contains the entire process of programme-making in a loop of interconnected facilities. Two structures rise from a common production platform that is partly underground. One is dedicated to broadcasting, the second to research and education. Management services are housed in the bridging section. Although most of the building is private, members of the public can tour the building on a dedicated route that offers spectacular panoramas across the city and vertigo-inducing views down-wards through transparent glazed floor panels in the uppermost section.

This building is a continuous box-shaped tube formed from an L-shaped ground section and two towers that lean towards each other at an angle of six degrees and are connected at the top by an L-shaped bridge. The surface of the tube is the primary structure and the floor plates act as internal stiffeners. This structure uses less steel than a conventional tower with the same floor area. High-performance glazing — with an integrated layer of expanded metal mesh that acts as a sunshade — is supported by a grid of diagonal steel tubes. The greater the structural stress on a particular part of the building, the greater the number of steel tubes in the grid, resulting in the facade's crazy-paving effect.

1   Buildings in context
2   View of CCTV with TVCC in background
3   Detail of facades
4   View of CCTV upwards from ground level
5   Exterior from street, TVCC in foreground
6   View from CCTV
7   Detail of CCTV exterior

3

4

5

Section through site

Site plan

6

7

National Stadium
Herzog & de Meuron

The National Stadium was the centrepiece of the 2008 Olympic Games. Here Herzog & de Meuron, in collaboration with the Chinese artist Ai Weiwei, continued to develop their interest in the skin of buildings, which they had explored earlier in another stadium design — the Allianz Arena (2005). The result is a dramatic undulating bowl composed from a network of mutually supporting diagonal columns, which rise from the ground to encase the solid central core of the stands. This purely structural exterior has earned it the nickname the 'Bird's Nest'.

A tangled lattice of silver-coloured steel beams tilts outwards from the ground and curves up over the stands. Some of the diagonals conceal and support stairs up to the different levels while the rising and falling rim of the bowl follows the line of ramps leading to the topmost stands. The crisscrossing horizontal, diagonal and vertical paths of access provide multiple promenading and meeting places, which are intrinsic to the Chinese way of life. There is also further space for socializing in the new, surrounding park, where echoes of the design of the stadium facade can be found in the patterns of the slate paths.

The stadium has a capacity of 80,000 (raised to 91,000 for the Olympics). An almost circular bowl-like shape helps to generate crowd excitement. The concrete tiers and attached facilities such as restaurants, shops and lavatories are painted red. The running track is also red and it seems to merge into the red seating on the lower levels. As the tiers rise, the red seats are gradually replaced by white ones, so that the top ranges blend into the white roof. The roof is weatherproofed with a transparent plastic membrane of ETFE (ethylene tetrafluoroethylene), with a sound-deflecting PTFE (polytetrafluoroethylene) fabric on the inner face to conceal the structure.

1,2 Exterior views of building
3 View of interior showing seating and track
4 Detail of steel lattice structure
5,6 Public circulation areas
7 Stadium in use
8 Entrance to lift

4

5

6

7

8

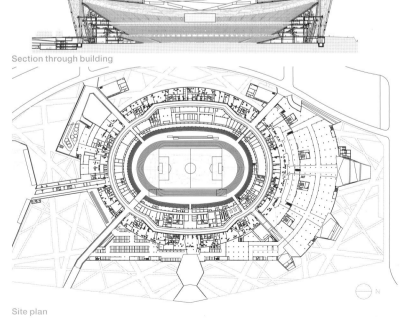

Section through building

Site plan

Iberê Camargo Foundation
Siza Vieira Arquiteto

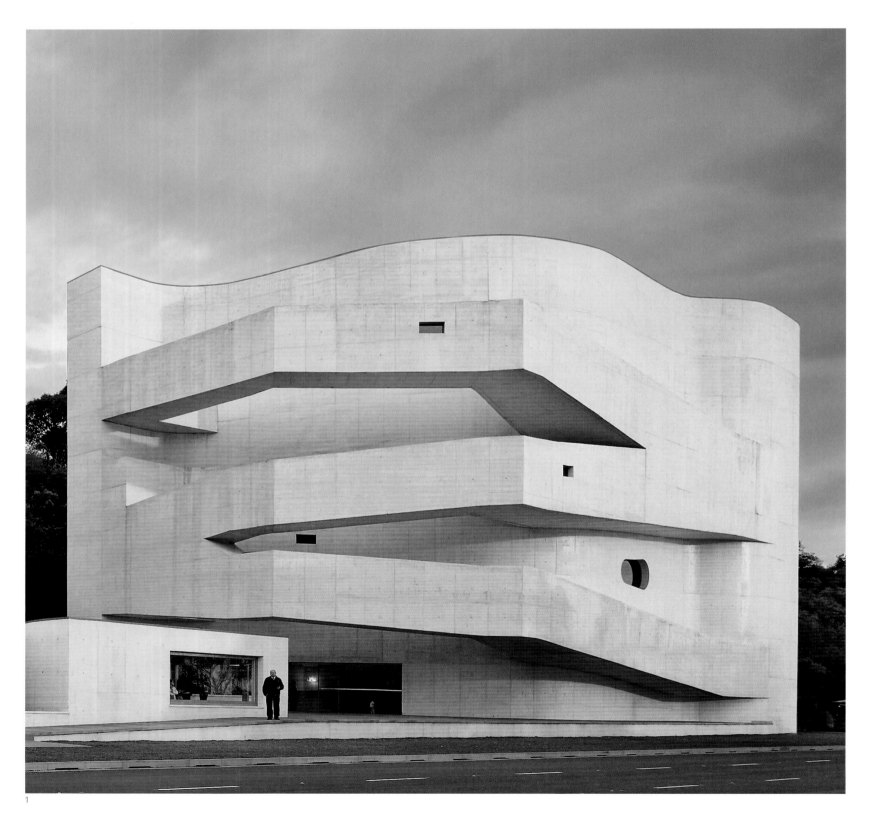

2

Porto Alegre, Brazil
2008

This new art gallery houses the work of Brazilian artist Iberê Camargo, and acts as a cultural centre hosting temporary exhibitions, workshops and lectures. A lush green cliff provides the backdrop and the river Guaíba runs in front of it. Álvaro Siza has separated the practical functions from the gallery spaces, placing them in two low blocks and the basement, while the galleries have a prominent position in a large four-storey block.

The building is both simple and complex. While the architecture is bold, with its extraordinary white concrete cliff-like street front and enclosed ramps weaving in and out of it, the purpose of the building is, above all else, to take the visitor on a journey to discover Camargo's work. From the street, visitors walk up a ramp to the café, shop, library, workshops and a lecture theatre arranged on and within the plinth. After passing beneath the angular bands containing the ramps, they reach the main entrance. The foyer is directly behind the wavy front wall and the ramps wind up, out of and around the full height of the space to the galleries above. The galleries are arranged over three floors and are divided into nine rooms that can be partitioned off to create different exhibition spaces.

The monolithic white concrete structure has no internal columns, the walls support the entire load. Wood floors provide a strong contrast to the white walls and ceilings. Siza designed all of the furniture, which is also made of wood. A small number of openings in the walls offer controlled views out, but in the main this is an introspective building. It is like a giant sculpture, or an Art Deco monument radically remodelled for the current century.

1   North facade
2   Entrance foyer
3   Sequence of looping ramps
4   Detail of entrance foyer
5,6 Details of interior ramps
7   Gallery space

3

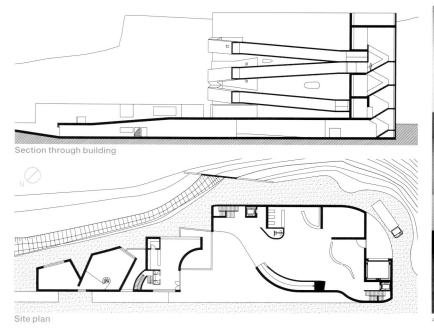

Section through building

Site plan

4

Porto Alegre, Brazil
2008

5

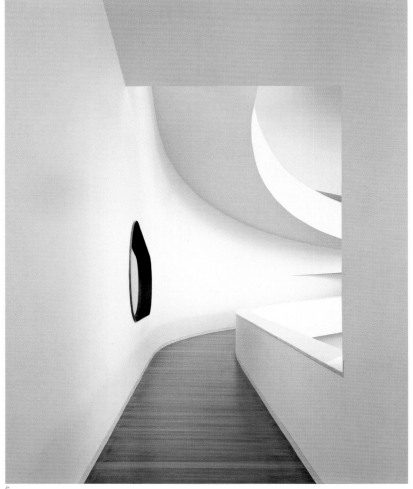

6

7

Index

Picture credits
Philippe Ruault: pp.6–9, pp.82–85, pp.114–117, Luís Asin: pp.10–13,
Rpbw: p.14, Andy Ryan: pp.18–21, Satoru Mishima: pp.22–25,
Getty Images: pp.26–29, Christian Richters: pp.30–33, pp.98–101,
© Katsuhisa Kida: pp.34–37, Helene Binet: pp.38–41, Roland Halbe:
pp.38–41, pp.46–49, Thomas Mayer: p.48, Nigel Young_Foster+Partners:
pp.50–53, Fernando Guerra & Sergio Guerra, FG+SG–Fotografia de
Arquitectura: pp.54–57, pp.154–157, Mitsuo Matsuoka: pp.58–61,
© H Helfenstein: pp.62–65, Stephane Compoint: p.66, Ben Johnson:
pp.66–69, Corbis: p.67, Duccio Malagamba: pp.70–73, p.78, Jan Bitter:
pp.74–77, Corbis: pp.78–81, Allianz Arena/B. Ducke: pp.78–81, Rob
Hoekstra: pp.82–85, Tamsyn Williams: p.86, Courtesy of the Eden
Project: pp.86–89, Marc Hill/Apex: p.87, Nick Gregory/Apex: p.89,
© Foundation Memorial to the Murdered Jews of Europe/Yara Lenke:
p.90, © Foundation Memorial to the Murdered Jews of Europe/Laubner:
p.90, © Foundation Memorial to the Murdered Jews of Europe/
Lepkowski: p.91, p.93, © Neil Emmerson/Robert Harding World Imagery/
Corbis: p.92, Katsuisha Kida: p.95, Lyndon Douglas: p.94, Rogers Stirk
Harbour+Partners: pp.94–97, Redshift Photography: p.97,
Architekturphoto: pp.102–105, Schaulager® Münchenstein/Basel,
Herzog & de Meuron, Architekten, Photo: Tom Bisig, Basel: p.105 [7],
Schaulager® Münchenstein/Basel, Herzog & de Meuron, Architects,
Photo: Heinrich Helfenstein, Zurich: p.102 [2], Jeroen Musch: pp.106–109,
Amparo Garrido: p.110, Roland Halbe/AENA: pp.111–112, Manuel Renau/
AENA: p.113, Antje Quiram: pp.122–123, p.125, Roger Frei: p.124, Roland
Tännier: pp.123–125, Toyo Ito & Associates, Architects: pp.126–129,
Jongoh Kim designhouse Inc.: pp.130–133, Photography (c) Yong–Kwan
Kim: pp.134–137, Richard Schlagman: p.140 (3) p.141 (6), Thomas Mayer:
pp.138–141, Iwan Baan: pp.146–153, ERICH SCHLEGEL/Staff
Photographe/Dallas Morning News/Corbis: p.153, Leonardo Finotti:
pp.154–157

Phaidon Press Limited
Regent's Wharf
All Saints Street
London N1 9PA

Phaidon Press Inc.
180 Varick Street
New York, NY 10014

www.phaidon.com

© 2009 Phaidon Press Limited

ISBN: 978 0 7148 5600 1

A CIP catalogue record for this book is available
from the British Library.

Text by Sally Watson and Justine Sambrook
Designed by Hans Stofregen
Printed in China